BUDGET AND GROW RICH

First edition. June 2, 2016.

Written by JD Lovil.

Budget and Grow Rich

Get more value for your money

JD Lovil

Budget and Grow Rich
Copyright © 2016 J D Lovil.

PUBLISHED BY:
JD Lovil Publishing

DISCLAIMER:

Budget and Grow Rich is an attempt by the Author to explain to the Reader the value of a budget, and how to construct a budget, using the same methods that the Author used to construct his own current budget. The Author does not claim any special training or expertise in the financial field.

1. Why a Budget?

Do you find that you have too much month left at the end of your money? If you do, perhaps you should take the advice of those people who have told you that you need a budget. I know what you are going to say. They have told you that you need a budget, but they never bothered to tell you how to make a budget. I am going to tell you how.

A budget needs to be an actual 'numbers on paper' type of thing. You cannot just mentally carry a budget around in your head, and expect to get some results. A budget is a daily 'record and check' your numbers process. You need to be able to record where your money comes from, when it comes, and where it goes. If you do not know these things, then you will never preserve your money for those lean days that we all potentially have.

Three types of action make a good budget. You need to know what things you spend your money on, and how much money you have coming in to spend, and you need to make a system that tracks that spending process, and lets you know where you stand at all times, in the process. The third part is that you need to track that spending each day that you buy things, so that you always have an accurate record of your spending.

In this chapter, we are going to find the baseline for your spending habits, tell you how to determine what categories of spending you need to have in your budget to get where you need to go, and find out what your actual spending history is, versus what you think it is.

I know what you are thinking. 'I don't have enough money coming in to meet my expenses. Do you really think that a budget is going to help me meet those expenses, and maybe allow me to save a little bit for a rainy day?' Yes, I do.

It is a natural result for people to spend any money that they have, which is not already allotted for some other expense. How many people do you know that will spend all the money in their pocket on lottery scratchers, even though they do not have enough money to pay their rent the next week?

Think of your budget as a trip you are about to take, and the money as the gasoline that will get you there. You need a roadmap in order to find your way to where you want to go, so that you do not wind up on the side of the road, out of gasoline. This is where a written budget comes into play. Since we live in modern times, I propose that you should create an Excel spreadsheet for this purpose. If you do not have Excel, there are multiple other free spreadsheets, such as Openoffice. They all generally work the same way.

Your budget should do a number of things for you. It should make you understand where your money is going. It should allocate money for each expense you must pay for, and a little money for those fun things that you need to enjoy life. It should anticipate expenses that do not come every month, such as insurance premiums, car or other repairs, trips, and that sort of things.

In order to create a livable budget, you will need to track your actual expenses for a little while, to determine where your money is actually going. You will also need to sit down, and list the amounts and types of other expenses that you anticipate will come along later, such as the repairs that I previously mentioned.

Once you have a list of the places that your actual money is going, and of future expenses, it is time to put a little bit of thought into how you can improve the spending process, to get you what you want to get, without hurting yourself.

Your vices, such as tobacco, coffee, alcohol, and even illegal drugs, need to be on your budget, but you need to rein in those items for which more is not better. You do not need to scratch five lottery tickets every day. One will bring you the same joy, and is statistically more likely to be a winner. Buying more of your food at the grocery store, and less at the convenience store is less expensive, and probably healthier.

A budget is not about depriving yourself. It is about spending your money more efficiently. A budget should account for covering all your needs, and as many of your desires as is practical, given the money available. It is also about allowing you to accumulate some savings, so that when you need to spend money, in an emergency, you can have the money to do what you need to do.

If you have hobbies, or vices, which you do not want to give up, then you need to figure them into your budget. If you budget carefully, you will be able to afford more of the things that you want to have, not less, and you will get more benefit from what you purchase.

In the next chapter, we will show you how you get the information that you need to put a good budget together. I guarantee that you will find that you can afford more of the things you want with a budget in hand, not less. It really is going to be great. Once you get use to using a budget, you will feel more in control of your money and spending than you ever have before. That is a very good feeling, indeed.

2. Tracking

In order to put your budget together, you need to understand your current spending habits. Each of us has unique patterns of spending money, and these patterns are determined by circumstances, our personalities, and our expectations of life.

Some of us go through life with no expectation of ever saving any money for a rainy day. If we have five hundred dollars, we always spend all five hundred dollars, or maybe, even more.

If you want to get off the 'spend it all the worst way' train, then you need a budget. In order to create the budget, you need to know how much of your income should go to each thing that you need to purchase in a given month. Since you are a real human being, with a unique spending pattern, you need to track how you usually spend your money, with no budget. I suggest that you do this for a month starting now.

For the next month, take something to write on wherever you go. Every time you spend money, write down the item you bought, and the amount you paid for it, and where you bought it. Make a difference between 'food from grocery store', and 'food from the convenience store', and other obvious distinctions. Note where the item is an unusually expensive item, and note (if you can tell), why you bought it. Were you hungry when you bought that grocery store item, or were you depressed when you bought that whiskey, candy and lottery ticket? Start thinking about eating before you grocery shop, or finding something active to do when you are down instead of buying stuff.

If you use a pocket notebook to record your expenses in the test month, dedicate the first page of the notebook to a list of category names to add to each item, so that you can easily sort them out at the end of the test, when you are adding up the results. For instance, tag a cigarette purchase with 'cig', a doctor's co pay with 'Health', food with 'F', and so forth. You can specify source with a hyphenation, such as food from the grocery store as F-Gr, and food from the convenience store as F-Con. You get the idea.

Now that you have numbers coming out of your ears, it is time to discuss another set of numbers that you need to consider. There are things that will happen in the future that are not typical monthly expenses. Some of these things are things like car repairs and maintenance, buying large items that you have to save for, or buy on credit, and emergencies both large and small.

I typically pay my automobile insurance once a year, avoiding that little five dollar per payment charge that they tack on to the price of insurance when you pay monthly. This yearly expense needs to be on my monthly budget, so that I have saved up the premium by the time I need to pay again. I know that you have things that are similar to list. Everybody does have something.

Let us assume that you tracked your expenses for a full month, and you spent gobs of money in these categories for the month:
- Rent of $600
- Electric power of $102.29
- Telephone $80.34
- Internet/cable of $125
- Food of $168.91
- New television of $204.25
- Miscellaneous household items of $226
- Books for $28.46
- Outings for $153
- Casino loss of $316
- Gasoline for $52
- Car payment of $225

- Car insurance of $75
- Health insurance of $227
- Doctor co pays of $30
- Out of pocket of $417

This comes to a total of $3030.25. Unfortunately, you only made $3028.99. Fortunately, you have a girlfriend, who has a four-year-old son, who has a piggy bank, which you raided for $1.27 during the month when you were short of funds. This left you with one penny in your pocket at the end of the month. Success!

There are a number of inclusions in this expenditure list that needs to be explained. Household items include such staples as toilet tissue and cleaning products, staples, and ink pens. I propose that the new television be included as a Household item in the final budget, since it is an household expense.

I am also going to suggest that the books, outings, and casino loss be included as Entertainment in the final budget, since they are entertainments. The fact that over half of the book expense was for porno magazines supports that idea. The category of 'Out of Pocket' included $116 worth of cigarettes and booze, and also $49.26 worth of DVDs. Let us call that $116 worth of Vices and add the $49.26 to Entertainment.

In the next chapter, we are going to start composing a rough draft of what your budget needs to be

3. Budget Planning

There are five categories of expenses that I think needs to be added to your budget that are not reflected in 'last month's expenses'. One is debt repayment, and the another is clothing. I also propose that you need a solid savings category, and an emergency fund and a Hedge category as well. Let me explain what these all mean.

While you may not have debt to be repaid at the moment, due to a credit score that is too low to get a credit card, you may want credit in the future. One easy way to start the ball rolling is to get a 'secure' card, which is a card that has a credit level equivalent to the amount of money you have deposited into a secure account with the credit card company. This is different from a debit card, because you do not draw money automatically from the account, unless you miss a payment. This sets up a record of credit transactions, which helps to raise your credit score.

The money you designate as debt repayment can be used to create the secured account, and then can be used to pay the minimal purchases you use the card to pay for. I would suggest that this should be allotted 1% of your net income.

Since you are a young male with the fashion sense of a gorilla, you should be able to spend another 1% of your income and be happy with the wardrobe you get for the money. I will also suggest that you need to put 5% of your income into a category called Hedge. Hedge money is used to supplement other category monies, where you zero the balance, but the expenditure is required to live, like rent, utilities, or transportation.

Emergency money is just what it sounds like, a nest egg for emergency situations, such as the loss of income, or major catastrophes. I suggest that you should devote another five percent of your income in this category.

The most important category for any budget is Savings. This is money that you need to live on when you retire, or when you hang up your spurs and go fishing for the rest of your life, also known as retirement for the common man. This should be ten percent of everything that you receive for the rest of your life, and it should be considered untouchable by you, no matter what, until the gray years.

Another category that you might consider adding is for vacations, or for major improvements in your life, such as starting a business. It is a debatable category, as it may also be apportioned from each of the other categories, as an expense that is valid to each of the categories.

Now, we are beginning to cobble together the framework for a budget. This is what we have so far:

Savings10%

Emergency5%

Hedge5%

Clothing1%

Debt Repay1%

Rent and Utilities600+102.29+80.34+125

Food$168.91

Household items $226+204.25

Entertainment$28.46+153+49.26

Vices$316+116

Transportation$52+225+75

Health $227+30

Miscellaneous $251.74

We know that you made a total of $3028.99 last month, so we will assume that to be your total income every month. Let us convert the amounts of each category used into percentages of income, and see how much we run over one hundred percent:

Savings10%

Emergency5%

Hedge5%

Clothing1%

Debt Repay1%

Rent and Utilities30%

Food5.6%

Household items 14.2%

Entertainment7.6%

Vices14.6%

Transportation11.7%

Health 8.5%

Miscellaneous 8.3%

This yields a total percentage of income of 122.57%. Yikes! We did add 22% of additional categories on top of the total tabulated expenses for last month. This means 22.5% of the proposed budget has to be cut where it can be cut. Transportation, Health, Food and Rent and Utilities cannot be messed with much, and Savings, Emergency, Hedge, clothing, and debt repayment is fixed, so that leaves us with Miscellaneous, Entertainment, Vices and Household to find the overages in, and make the budget equal 100% of income.

The television was an extraordinary expense, so most of the $204.25 that you paid for it can be backed out of Household expenses. Budget fifty per month for replacements, such as breakdown of appliances. What kind of fool sits and loses $316 in the casino? Figure that you should have walked when you were down $100, and walk that $216 extra out of Vices. You also spent over a hundred per week on Miscellaneous out of pocket expenses. Reduce that by about $40 per week, and you still have plenty for snack foods and the Big Gulps you like so much.

Vices14.6%-$216=14.6-7.2=7.4%

Miscellaneous 8.3%-$(40*4)=8.3-5.3=3%

Household items 14.2%-154.25=14.2-5.1=9.1%

We have just found 7.2+5.3+5.1= 17.6% of the 22.5% we need to trim. That leaves 4.9% left to trim out of the budget. It is time to get hardcore. A quick calculation reveals that 4.9% is $148.48 of your income. I do not want to trim more of the out of pocket money, since you will have it to buffer your other expenses when needed, so that leaves Vices and Household to trim. I suggest that we trim 2% from Vices, and reduce the alcohol intake and porno. Then let us reduce the Household budget by 2.9%, which brings us to our 100% budget.

Savings10%

Emergency5%

Hedge5%

Clothing1%

Debt Repay1%

Rent and Utilities30%

Food5.6%

Household items 6.2%

Entertainment7.6%

Vices5.4%

Transportation11.7%

Health 8.5%

Miscellaneous 3%

Once we have a final budget, you may find that your spending changes enough to merit a modification of the allotments to each category. This is okay, if the expenses maintain a consistency that makes it useful, but do not be too fast about changing your future budget. Your unconscious mind will play games with your behavior for short periods of time, to get you to free up money that it wants to blow.

4. Structures

Now that you have a tentative budget, you need to create the infrastructure that it describes. You can use a budget for an 'all cash' situation, but it is more feasible for the numbers that your budget comes up with to be the same as the balance that your checking, savings, or other account, where you get your pay check deposited.

Let us say that you have a central checking account, where your paycheck is automatically deposited. If you withdraw money from the account, to put it in your pocket for the Miscellaneous expenses, you account for it as an expenditure in the Miscellaneous column. The total on you budget will always reflect the money in the account. If you withdraw the money in a complicated process, you can always create a secondary 'cash only' budget to track your expenses.

Let me tell you how I use my budget. I have a checking account in the bank down the road from me, into which my income is automatically deposited. If I withdraw pocket money for the week, I subtract the money from the appropriate columns, and I put the money in carefully marked envelopes, until I spend it for the items for which I withdrew it.

When the balance of a particular category, such as Savings, becomes large enough, I transfer the money to a savings account with Ing Direct, or a interest bearing checking account with Ally Bank, or in the case of Savings, usually straight into one of my IRAs. Any money transferred out of the central account is also subtracted from the appropriate columns, but it is transferred into an account that is clearly labeled with the category name, such as R&U, Transportation or other category. Needless to say, money from the R&U checking account is only used to pay for rent or utilities.

We are describing a habit here. You will have to get into the habit of documenting your expenditures on your budget, which will be hard for you to do, every time, but once you get the habit, it will be very easy. You will wonder why you never did a budget before. You may even find that you keep track of your friend's money in your head, and cringe when they make a stupid error in judgment with their money.

In the next chapter, we are going to start working on making the spreadsheet of the budget. Relax. It will be fun!

5. The Spreadsheet

In addition to the categories, you want a budget that gives you a place to record the date of the transaction, and a description of that transaction. You also want a place that reflects the balance of money available in your budget. I suggest that you want the budget spreadsheet to be about 100 rows of transactions, so that you do not feel cramped, trying to get too much information into too small a place.

Let us start by opening a new workbook in Excel. I am going to assume that you have at least a small amount of experience with manipulating applications such as Word, Excel, and other useful files on your Personal Computer. If you get lost, you may need to take a class or something, to introduce you to the twenty-first century.

Excel is composed of cells, in which you can set the rules. You can format how text or numbers appear in the cells, and you can have the cell perform mathematical or logic operations on the numbers or text as you wish. You set those parameters by left clicking on a cell, right clicking, and then left clicking on the choice of 'format cell'.

Close your eyes, and visualize what I tell you. I used the format function to label columns of cells with the category tags, create borders of the cells, and created different color fill colors, in order to keep on track. I set the general appearance format for the body of the budget. The bottom cells, from C101 all the way across to R101, I designed the bottom cells of the columns, which will calculate the current total of each category at each point in time, and in S101, an equation will give us the cumulative total cell for the entire budget spreadsheet. I have not yet set the functions that control the actual numbers that we will insert into the cells.

You cannot tell with your eyes closed, but I also took the opportunity to align the text or numbers I enter into the cells in the center of the cell, so that they do not crowd one side of the cell. That is another of the format functions.

We want the spreadsheet to do certain things, so we do not have to do them ourselves. First, when we receive income, we want to record the number in column C, and have the spreadsheet calculate and enter the appropriate amount under each category in the cell in that column that is appropriate. You make it do this by putting a function into the cell. We will use the Save category to demonstrate this fun function.

Save is supposed to get ten percent, or 0.1 of total net income. If we left click on a cell in the Save column, say cell D4, we can put an equation in the header at the top of the page, just to the right of the symbol for function fx. The function will reference the cell where you would input the income, which is C4, and it would look like this:

$$=C4*0.1$$

Therefore, after setting that up, you can enter a 1000 figure into C4, and D4 will instantly show 100, which is 10% of 1000. Try it!

Adjusting the equation to reflect the different percentages that the budget is supposed to put into each category, you can go all the way across one row to have a set of cells that will instantly calculate the appropriate amounts to put into each cell, based on the income you put into cell C4.

Once you have one validly formatted cell in each column, you can copy and paste them in every body cell in that column, and the function will adjust to the correct numbered 'C' cell as needed.

It may be helpful to freeze the top row of cells in place, allowing the body of the budget to scroll up, while keeping the label for the column in sight. You can do this by selecting the view tab, and clicking on the Freeze pane tab, then selecting freeze top row. That way, you do not have to keep scrolling up to figure out which category you are working with.

I constructed my spreadsheet with rows one, two, and three for Categories, Percentages, and Balance forward, respectively. First and second rows do not figure into any calculations that you want the budget to make, but you will need to have row three, since the amounts that you bring forward when you refresh your budget is part of the amounts in each category. You should be refreshing your spreadsheet each month, or when the spreadsheet is nearly full, by copying an unused cell in each of the categories, and pasting to all the cells from rows 4 to 100, after bringing the legacy total from the bottom of the column to the cell on row 3.

You can get the last row of cells (in row 101 of this budget) to show the total value for each category by using another function equation in the format of:

$$=SUM(D3:D100)$$

for the cells on column D. You can do this for the rows C through R in this particular spreadsheet, substituting the appropriate letter for the cells in each column. This equation will calculate the total value for all the numbers in that column. If you have 2+16+3-9 (four entries, three positive numbers, and one negative), you will see the number 12 in cell D101.

Once you have completed putting the appropriate version of this equation into each of the cells on row 101 from C101 to R101, you can make the single cell S101 show the value in the whole budget account by inputting this equation into the cell:

$$=D101+E101+F101+G101+H101+I101+J101+K101+L10
1+M101+N101+O101+P101+Q101+R101$$

You can make an endless number of improvements or tweaks to the spreadsheet, but this one ready to use now. When you put income into Column C, the numbers will be calculated and inserted into the correct cells. You can also manually insert values into any cell, reflecting additions or subtractions of funds. When you take money out, or pay out, you enter the number, with a minus sign in front of it, and the budget will subtract that money from the budget total.

When money is surplus in one of the categories, you know that you can transfer the money to a savings account at https://secure.capitalone360.com (the current location of Ing Direct), or an interest bearing checking account at https://www.ally.com/.

Let us wrap this book on budgets up with a look at important considerations. Check out the next chapter!

6. Tracking

You need to be dedicated to maintaining your budget up to date, and with every transaction shown. Do not start cheating on the budget. Budgets get mad, and then they plot their revenge. Their revenge consists of making sure that you stay poor, and never, ever keep any of the money you make.

Again, let me stress this point. Track every transaction, and stick with the budget limits. A man with a budget is always richer than the man without a budget.

7. Sustain the Budget

Here are the obligatory Dos of budgeting. Do not let your participation in the budget process lapse. Follow your budget religiously. If a category of your budgeted income runs out of money, practice acting broke. Do not spend money out of a different category. That way lays hell and damnation.

The End

JD Lovil

Writes both nonfiction and fiction books. He is the writer of several How-To and speculative nonfiction books, as well as several cross genre science fiction novels, dealing with the existence of a multitude of parallel earths as required by the Many Worlds interpretation of Quantum Theory. Originally from Arkansas, JD Lovil now lives in Phoenix, Arizona. Visit his website at

www.Jdlovil.jimdo.com

If you enjoyed this book, please consider leaving a favorable Five Star review at the site where you purchased it.

You may connect with the Author on Facebook at:
https://www.facebook.com/jd.lovil.9

You may also connect with the Author on Pinterest:
http://www.pinterest.com/jdlovil9

You may also connect with the Author by email at
jdlovilpublishing@gmail.com

If you enjoyed this book, you may also enjoy
<u>Whacking Happiness</u>
Here is an excerpt of that book for you:
Chapter Seven of
Whacking Happiness

Chapter 7: Belief is Reality

Let me say something that you might not have ever realized. Beliefs are expectations, and expectations are beliefs. They are the two faces of the same coin. If you *believe* in a god who grants prayers, then you also *expect* that you will receive the answer to the prayer you just prayed.

Whatever you expect the world to be for you, that is a belief. If you believe that you do not deserve good outcomes for your activities, then this will also be your expectation. This is what the Undermind sees. What the Undermind sees is what it will always deliver.

Let us take an example to illustrate this point. Let us say that you are one of those hedonistic infidel non-Christians out in the world that may have an abstract thought of a belief in a god of some sort, somewhere out there. Then one day, you are in an emotional slump, and a traveling Preacher starts to make sense to you.

The Preacher man tells you that you can be saved if you just accept Jesus, and then he drones on and on about the doing of this, quoting endless verses and painting mental pictures of hellfire and angel wings. This starts to sound like the most positive idea in your life right then, and you reach a point where you realize that you actually believe in the idea that Jesus can save you.

Once you have that belief, you start to see the world around you in a different way. New difficulties in Life become tests of your faith. Some of the agony of life melts away, as you have mentally given many of the responsibilities of life to this Jesus person, and so your worries are diminished.

As you go along with this belief in mind, you start to notice that the world around you seems to be confirming the truth of this belief, and your experiences start to be put in the 'Pro Jesus' pile of experiences. The more confirmations you get of the validity of the belief, the more you become sure of it, and the surer you become of the belief, the more the world shows you confirmations of it. This simple feedback loop comes courtesy of the ability of your Undermind to manipulate your reality, and of course of your ability to screen your sensory input to support your worldview.

As you might have discerned from my previous diatribe, I do not actually believe that humans possess Free Will. I approach this issue from several directions. I then ruin my own argument by advocating that we need to act as though we do have Free Will, and distinguish between what I call Absolute and Practical Free Will.

On a metaphysical level, if anyone (including an omniscient god) knows exactly what the future holds for us, it means that the future is fixed. We cannot have Free Will in a world where we must fulfill a fixed future.

On a physical level, our choices are made in a world where our past experiences, and our inherited gifts and traits, and the mental programming that all of these influences have built will define what choice we will make in any decision process. In other words, a sufficiently intelligent observer who is unnaturally familiar with all of the components that built our personality will be able to discern each choice that we will make before we have made it.

From a psychological standpoint, I have come to understand that our identity is a thin veneer upon the aggregate of our mind. While we run an endless routine in the Beta state that defines our person as distinct from all other parts of the world, the rest of our mind does not. The Undermind feels no need to separate the Self from the rest of the universe, and so the larger part of your mind does not self-identify. When you sleep, you maintain your point of view in dreams, but it is arguable as to whether you maintain your sense of self. One must be a distinct individual in order to exercise Free Choice.

Now that I have argued against the concept of what I call 'Absolute Free Will', I must define some logical argument, which allows me, as the Author, and you, as the Reader, assume that our attempts at change are not an exercise in futility. For this, I bring in my concept of 'Practical Free Will'.

If someone attacks me with intent to kill me, I must act as if the attacker deserves whatever harm my defense does to him, even if I assume that he actually has no control over his actions. If it gets to court, I must assume that he is functionally responsible *enough* for his actions to deserve his prison sentence, because I need to justify the right to lock him away from the helpless population.

While God or a sufficiently intelligent observer may be able to determine my every future action, I must assume that my sensation of having Free Will is a practical Truth. I am distinguishing it as *practical* because it results in my accepting as rational and reasonable what happens in my life. I need some sense of *meaning* in my life, and in order to have that sensation of meaning, I must have a set of experiences that make sense to me.

Our set of inherited and experience-influenced modes of action behaviors are complex enough that one would be unaware of the lack of Free Will in the choices we make, if we did not resort to the philosophical reasoning process. We may as well *act as if* we do indeed possess Free Will.

It is important for the person seeking a happy life to have a consistent and beneficial set of beliefs to support the goal of happiness. In order for us to understand what subjects of our lives the beliefs should address, we need to briefly examine the various aspects of life that tends to affect our happiness.

These aspects come in two major sections. The first section is the set of experiences, inheritances and circumstances which have a significant effect on our happiness. The second section is how we react to our experiences, how we see ourselves, and (basically) the decision that we have made as to whether we are winners or losers in the game of life.

I have been around for a few decades, and this is what I have learned. For every opportunity that I have had and taken advantage of, there are a thousand which I did not take. For every woman that I have had a relationship with, there are a thousand that I did not. Life is like that. I have many regrets for the things that I did not have for each choice I have made, whether it was a good one or a bad one.

How you choose to react to such regrets is entirely up to you. The lesson to be learned is that there is no such thing as too much experience, good or bad. It is the stuff of which a full life is made. We can rejoice in the pleasures that we have received from life, or we can lament all of the things that we did not get.

The amount of good experiences you can get in the living is huge, but no matter how hard you try, you can never do, be, or receive *everything*. This is where the perfectionist fails. In the perfect life, you could have it all, but since you can't, there are no perfect lives. It might be that you could settle for a good life instead.

If you look closely, you will see that all of your experiences, even the ones that hurt, will teach you valuable lessons, if you are willing to learn. If you had an abusive parent, the lesson might be that you should not believe what they tell you about yourself. Such a parent is self-absorbed, and he or she knows only themselves. If they say something abusive to you, you can be sure that they believe that thing about themselves, and are projecting it onto you.

How we react to those experiences we have is the province of what we choose to believe, and the person we choose to be. There are two ways that one can tailor their beliefs into a set that helps them live a happy life. The first way is to decide on the best set of beliefs, and then go about a long series of procedures to cement them into your personality.

The second method takes a little preamble to explain. It still involves picking good beliefs to have, but there is a shortcut to making them fit you. It has to do with something that you already do, but you may not realize it.

When you start a new activity in your life, such as going to school, playing a sport, or starting a new job, you always do a most unusual thing to make it work. Before you start the new activity, you decide what sort of person you need to be to do that activity, and you create a new Persona.

Think about it. You are not the same person at work that you are at home. At work you are active and productive, and you never *ever* pick your nose in front of your coworkers. At home, you deal with your family or your pet in ways you would *never* deal with your coworkers, and the best relationship you have there is *not* with your boss, it is with your favorite easy-chair.

You create this new personality to deal with the new situation with only a vague and almost unconscious understanding of what you need to be for the activity. You succeed in that activity almost solely on how well you have crafted your new personality. Your actual skills and abilities have much less of an effect on your success than your new personality does. If you put only a slightly greater effort into *creating* the personality, you could cause a *huge* positive change in your outcome.

Why not use the same natural ability to create a new Persona to make your new successful and happy self. To create the new you, you need to decide what you *want* (your goals), decide **what you need to believe in**, and then use the tools that we put in your toolbox, including a new Persona, to make it all happen.

Your new beliefs should cover the areas of your life. You should have beneficial, spiritual, or other beliefs that adds to your sense of meaning and destiny in your life, a set of beliefs that covers your social, creative, financial, and any other beliefs that you can define which will solidify the happy life you so desire.

At this point, we should go over the process of goal setting. This will give you the general parameters that you should address in structuring your beliefs. The next chapter will cover that subject.

Also by JD Lovil

Non-Fiction
Becoming Libertarian
Lose Weight Naturally
Whacking Happiness
Unknown Visitors
Libertarian Survivalist
Fiction
Worldship Praxis
Shadow of Worlds
Vanguard of Man
Jigsaw World

Most of these books are available in paperback and audiobook formats, in addition to the digital format. All of the fiction is available in all three formats.

Don't miss out!

Click the button below and you can sign up to receive emails whenever JD Lovil publishes a new book. There's no charge and no obligation.

https://books2read.com/r/B-A-XMCC-CJUJ

Connecting independent readers to independent writers.

Did you love *Budget and Grow Rich*? Then you should read *Unknown Visitors* by JD Lovil!

Have you seen a flying saucer?

Have you ever wondered what they come here for?

I used to think that only odd people saw UFOs, but I have changed my mind.

\>>> People from all walks of life have reported them! They cannot all be wrong.

Why do all of the aliens reported appear humanoid? What do they want? Will they save us?

\>>> This is an attempt to answer those questions, or at least to ask the questions more usefully.

Learn the answers to these burning questions today!

Survive the coming alien invasion. Buy a copy of 'Unknown Visitors' today.